Dear You,

I want you to know that I see you.

I want you to know that even if no one else
does, even if you are a ghost in this
bookshop, or just the static floating across the
screen of your computer, wherever you're
reading this, I see you.

I see you in the dark, and I see you in the
gray. I see you as a story, as words I have
spoken or may yet speak. Maybe only in a
memory or a dream.

I want you to know that the space between the
letters in this book is a space for you.

So if you have the time and the inclination,
you can sit here with me, just for a while.

And perhaps between us, we can see the truth,
as it stands in these moments that we share.


—Iain S. Thomas

I

In which we fall in love.

## A Falling Bird

They love you like rain loves,
and in return, you love like a flood loves,
and just like a flood,
you are not in control
because that is the nature of your love,
and you have never learned to love
another way.

## A Door in Infinite

"Tell them how we met."

"I was knocking on your heart,
hoping that you were listening."

"And some empty part of me
heard them knocking
from the other side of the universe,
and I answered."

## An Admission

Be honest
and tell them what hurts.

Because if you don't,
you will never be happy.

## A Book Left Out in the Rain

Love is the wrong word,
even if it is the only word that makes
sense.

It is different. It is the kind of love
that someone puts in a book
and closes and opens,
like wings.

And like everything with wings,
it feels like it could fly away
at any moment.

And shake the air.

And leave both of us
breathless and stunned.

## A Star Shining On Forever

How long will this last?

If you mean the world,
or who we are to each other,
then I do not know.

If you mean how
long will I be me,
then my answer is
forever.

A Scratch in the Chrome

The heart is not a perfect machine
that you can make demands of.

It's just a heart.

Just a thing.

And somehow,
absolutely everything.

## A Broken Watch

Forever is the time
it takes for you to look at me
when you laugh in a crowded room.

## A Tree Growing Where It Can't

The sunlight says,
sometimes you fall in love
like snow falls at night,
quietly and gently
covering every part of you,
and the next day
the world looks completely different.

And that is how I fall in love.

Like snow.

## A Promise on a Bridge

Love me like you love me,
and I will love you like I love you.

If you let me be the person I am,
when you are far away
and you don't know what to do,
the thought of me will be a home for you.

A Single Beat of a Bird's Heart

Do not say,

"I love you,"

if you mean,

"You make my life easy."

Because love is only ever easy
in the beginning
and from then on,
if it's worth it,
it needs work.

So don't go into love thinking
it will be easy.

Go into love thinking
it will be worth the work.

## A Conversation the Next Day

I think I'm going to be hurt by you,
and if I'm going to be hurt by you,
I want you to do it accurately.
I want to understand it.
I want the hurt to be worth it.

## A Sudden Silence

Maybe your heart
has heard the same thing
for so long,
when it hears a voice
tell it something else is possible,
it is afraid.

## A Field of Wheat in the Wind

I ask only for forever,
and every single time
you answer me in some different way,
because every part of you
is the answer
I am looking for.

Let our lives be a question
and let us never stop answering it.

## A Soft Light on the Horizon

If the aliens landed and
wanted to know the most beautiful
word I knew, I would tell them your name.

I would tell them the name
of the town you grew up in.

I would tell them how your mother
whispered stories
to help you sleep
when you were a baby,
and how she would take you outside
and show you the moon as a way
to let you know
that there was an order
to things,
and even big things had their place,
even if that place was in the night sky
among the stars.

I would explain
that there is a way
you can touch me that does not feel
like anything else on Earth.

Not like water, or stone, or air, or fire.

I would say your name three times,
and I would say that your name
is all of these things
and it is the most beautiful word I know.

# A Place We Can Talk

"Is this it?"

"It's my heart."

"Is that all of it?"

"I don't know.
But everything feels different
when you hold me.
The world spins a little faster and
our days feel a little shorter.

The stars leave silvery trails behind them
as they arc across the sky above us.

The sun and the moon chase each other
when you hold me.

I am not myself and you are not you."

"Then who are we?"

"Maybe because we are nothing to no one,

we are everything to each other.

And this feeling,

I swear,

is my whole heart."

## A Child Collecting Leaves

I asked you what you missed the most
and you told me you missed the ocean.

So I filled every room in the house
with seashells until, at night,
you could hear a thousand waves
whispering you to sleep.

I asked you what you missed and
you told me you missed the forest.

So I filled the house with pine needles
until at night, when you closed your
eyes, you could smell a giant forest
all around you.

I asked you what you missed
and you told me you missed the stars.
So I took a screwdriver and
made a thousand holes in the roof.

I asked you what you missed and
you told me you missed kissing.
And so I kissed you.
And I kissed you.
And I kissed you.

I kissed you in
spring,
summer,
autumn,
winter.

I kissed you by the sea and
in the forest and
under the stars.

Because when I kissed you,
in those moments,
neither of us missed anything at all.

A Lottery Ticket in the Rain

Sometimes all it takes
to change your life forever
is a person you didn't know
you were looking for.

## A Dictionary

To look at you
is to want to invent a new word for love,
because the only word for love is love,
and when I look at you,
I feel like you deserve better.

## A Challenge

You took my tongue,
and so
I wrote about love.

## An Infinite Line

I am the start
of ten thousand
poems

but you are the end
of all of them.

## II

In which we are sad.

## An Empty Parking Lot

You won't see the good
in things because
they won't be perfect.

And you will starve
because you will have
no goodness in your life.

Because you are waiting for perfect.

And perfect never comes.

A Factory in the Sky

Your heart was too big.

They had to break it
to fit it inside your body
before you were sent to Earth.

A Shadow on the Water

You are carrying all that you are
like a bucket trying to hold the ocean,
spilling over and apologizing for it
because you were told to be small
and you never learned how to do that.

## A Word That Matters

I will see my reflection

in the screen

or I will notice it

as I pass a window

and I will remember

that I am not actually

who I think I am,

I'm just a person who too often

is afraid to go outside.


In words,

here,

is the only place

I've ever felt good enough.

A Sign of Indifference

We are not the same.

You do not wake up every morning
unsure of who you're supposed to be.

You've never had to take a moment
and negotiate your right to exist.

And I understand that
you do not understand
these things.

But I cannot be anyone else
but me.

## A Stranger on the Street

There are people who
are too sensitive for the world,
and their brain
gives them lines to say
that make no sense,
and all of the nonsense
and the fairy tales
and the strange light
of everything
goes into them.

And they are beautiful
in a way few
will ever know.

A Road to Somewhere I've Never Been

I don't think there's anyone else out there
who knows what it feels like to be me.

But maybe if I crumple part of myself
into a little ball
and throw it out of the car,
someone will pick it up one day and say,

"This is mine."

### A Chance to Run Home

To think that you are alone
in everything you feel
is to experience a kind of loneliness
that no one should ever know.

## A Bird Looking North

I am looking for all the places I cannot go.

The surface of the sun.

The other side of the moon.

A ship in a glass bottle.

Home.

## A Fire in a Forest

If you make anything sad enough
or true enough,
people will call it a poem.

They will see you spinning
in the afternoon light and celebrate you,
not knowing that you are a fire
burning down all around,
an explosion of sparks and orange leaves
walking the earth.

Sometimes, people lie to you,
because they just want to
break something good
to see what it looks like
when it shatters.

Sometimes, people are assholes
for no other reason
than they want to be assholes.

There is no magic
or mystery to assholes.

## A Noise in the Night

I am picked up by the wind
and I must believe
that if it is taking me somewhere,
it is taking me into the soft light
of the future,
to a place where I am not me but still me,
where I am only the parts of myself
that accept every other part of me.

## A Clock That Tells Strange Time

Sometimes

I just want someone

to put my heart

in a watchmaker's hands,

as a jumble of silver shards,

and say, "Fix it."

## An Unknown Color

There is a feeling
I do not have a name for,
and all my life,
I have been trying
to give it one.

A Rising Moon

How long must I wait to feel the way

I've been told I'm supposed to feel?

When am I allowed to feel
the way I feel?

An Absentee

I'm sorry for saying hello.

But you looked like a way out
of me.

A Horse Running

We're just born.

And we think we're not good enough.

So we chase something
to fill the empty space inside of us
with some kind of goodness.

Something that will make us well
enough
to hold ourselves again.

A Fish Out of Everything

I have decided
when I grow up,
I want to feel normal
in a crowded room.

## A Broken Television

We live in a world
in which people think
being angry
will make them feel better,
but instead,
it just makes them angry.

## Taillights in the Distance

I know

there is a part of the road

that does not have

this place in the rearview mirror.


And I will drive

until I get there.

## A Fading Star

I feel like if I could just take
one good step,
I could run forever.

## A Dog Running in the Street

They put clothes on you
that don't fit and say,

"You'll grow into this."

And one day you stop growing
and the world is still too big for you.

A Brief Spark

Somewhere, a band plays on.

A captain salutes a wave.

A starling arcs across the sky.

And I am the band
and I am the captain
and I am the starling,
arcing across the sky.

# A Bike Left Against a Tree

I feel like I've seen enough of the future
become the past to know
that what you're haunted by,
you will always be haunted by.

A circle of salt
couldn't even keep the wind at bay,
and a priest will mumble what he mumbles,
and his blessings will not be worth the
money you paid for them.

I'm not saying you can't change,
just that you can't change the things
that have happened to you.

You must grow around them, and
if you grow for long enough,
you can swallow them up,
like a tree swallows up a sign or bike
left leaning against it, decades ago.

Or maybe all you can do in the end
is make friends with your ghosts.

## An Empty Bench

Sometimes I sit on a bench
and I look at the people sitting around me,
and wonder if they're wondering who they are
as hard as I'm wondering who I am,
or who I'm supposed to be.

I try to think my way out of everything.

Sometimes I feel like
if I can just think better,
I can fix me.

But sometimes, I think
I'm just thinking too much.
Thinking about thinking.
Thinking about trying not to think.

And I am chased out of my own mind.

A Spinning Wheel

Don't worry.

This doesn't hurt.

This is just who I am.

## A Bag in a Doorway

Sometimes I forget to put my anxiety down
when I get home and I just carry it around
on my back all night
because it's familiar
and it feels strange to let it go.

## A Tree House in Winter

I feel like there was a meeting
before I was born
that I wasn't invited to.

I feel like there is a secret button
everyone has
somewhere on their body
that they can press
whenever they want to feel normal,
and I was never given one
or told where mine was.

## A Broken Telephone

I still wish I knew
what I was supposed to sound like.
But in the quiet at night,
sometimes I think I can hear me.

Or at least someone who sounds like me.

A Sense of Fear

I miss the world.

And the biggest room in it
would feel small right now.

### A Shiver

Some people do
so much
to be loved by others,
and so little
to love themselves.

## III

**In which one of us leaves.**

## A Shadow in a Flame

I love you.

I love you as much as I have ever loved you.

And some part of me will never, ever stop loving you.

But there is another part of me
that feels like we're trying to go somewhere
where we'll both be happy,
and that we're both always trying to get there,
and we're always trying really, really, really hard.

But I don't know if we'll ever get there.

I feel like we'll just always be trying.
And I'm tired.
And I need to know if you're tired too.

This doesn't mean I don't love you.

It means I love you enough to tell you
I don't know if I can try anymore.

## An Act of Forgiveness

Maybe,

they were some great lesson

that you needed to learn

and one day,

you will be able to look back,

and be glad that you learned it.

## A Ripple

Some part of you already knows
if you're going to leave
or not.

It is how you will be hurt and
how long you will be hurt for
that you are trying to decide.

## A Path Across a Field

I tried to write you out of me.

I tried to cut you out
the way you cut me out.

And nothing worked.

And now all I can do,
line
by
line,
is write myself out of me.

A Sad Goodbye

You left today
like rivers flowing backward.
The paths and waterways
connecting us
however small and insignificant
carried pain instead of love.

In the end, the lights go out
one by one and knowing they were lit
doesn't dim the dark.

A Long Drive Nowhere

I have driven so far
only to discover
you cannot outrun
a broken heart.

## A Door Slammed Off Its Hinges

Maybe you're a sad mess
and I'm a sad mess too,
and maybe right now,
this is just who we are.

Maybe that's all we can be
and all we can have right now.

And maybe, that can be enough.

## An Edge Where the Water Meets the Land

I still put the seashell to my ear
and pretend that the ocean
is my friend,
and she is whispering to me
about her day.

And sometimes,
I ask if she can put you on for a while,
but she never does.

A Broken Road Stretching into the Distance

I'm not saying
you didn't hurt me.

I'm saying
there is a part of me
that's willing to risk
being hurt again.

Just not by you.

(I don't think that's being strong.

I just think I'm carrying on.)

## Shadows in the Sky

Where is the music in your mouth
now that every bird has flown away?
Where is anything that matters anymore?

All gone.
All gone away.

## A Childhood Passing You By

And you know now,
there's a kind of quiet that only the quiet know.

And there's a kind of place
only the people without a place know.

### A Firework That Doesn't Light

I want to know
how many different ways to feel
are still written on your arms,
and am I still one of them?

## A Lonely Corner

You're trying
not to say something
because it's easier
to leave
than it is to talk.

## A Ticket to Anywhere Else

Some of us need to love deeply and earnestly.

Some of us need to feel like love
is painful in order to know that it is love.

Some of us just want to be
in the same room as someone else.

The question is not,
"Is their love enough for me?"
the question is,
"Is your love enough for you?"

## A Key Lost in a Field

Unless you are willing
to let someone else hold your hand
in the dark
and guide you out of yourself,
you will never be able to truly love
or be loved by anyone.

## A Flashlight in a Forest

I still walk the paths we used to walk,
hoping I can catch up to us and
tap us on the shoulder and say,

"Hold on to this,
because it doesn't last forever."

And my hand
would brush against yours
as I left.

## A Nothing

A beautiful bird in a cage eventually
becomes an empty cage and a dead bird
and a loss of words
and one wondering at a funeral
how many birds must fly away.

## An Overgrown Path

Maybe I was wrong.

You never gave me
a good enough reason for leaving.

And now all I can do
is think of all the reasons
why you could've left me.

And I just want you to know
that whatever your reason was,
you hurt me, and despite that,
I don't want to hurt you back.

You were good for a while.

I thought I was good too.

A Star Blinking Out

Say the good name you have for me,
that you hide from me.

Have the kind of fight you want
before one of us has to ask,
"Who started this?"

How do you win a fight
no one started?

And why even have it
when we've forgotten our
names.

A Catherine Wheel

"Tell me why you're leaving."

"Because I don't think
you know why you're staying."

### A Regret

Maybe you only get
one good thing in your life

and maybe if God
is feeling cruel that day,
he makes that thing
a person.

A Moment of Clarity

Give me a name
for the scar
you've given me.

And then tell me
this doesn't hurt.

Because
I can't say it back to you.

An Ice Cube at the Bottom of a Glass

Yes it hurts,
but it hurts because it was good,
and while I'm sorry it hurts,
I will not apologize for it being
good.

## A Sunset in a Foreign Country

I always thought

that we were meant to change together.

That somehow our seasons would line up,

that your spring and your summer

would become mine,

that we would share an autumn,

that I would be with you until the end of winter.


But everything changed.

And it changed without me.

## An Amber Leaf

Everyone has one love in their life
that changes them forever.

It shapes something inside them
and they are different for having loved.
Maybe you love other people along the way
and maybe you try to love other people afterward
but you know it's not the same
because you have tasted something
you cannot un-taste.

Maybe you're fourteen when you meet them
and maybe you're forty.

But you only get one.

That's what I know now.

Because I've tried to love other people,
and while I still love,
I do not love the same anymore.

A Burning Forest

God knows,
enough terrible things happened
to both of us when we were together.

Maybe he was punishing us for something.
Maybe what we had was too good.

Maybe you're not supposed
to have anything that good
while you're still alive.

A Prism

They left because
someone convinced them
that happiness
is a kind of person
you can find twice.

## A Window Rattling

You smell like apples
when you think of your childhood.
You smell like ash and smoke
when you think of your father.
You smell like shampoo
when you think of your mother.

When you looked at me,
and you were thinking of someone else,
you smelled like rain.

And I know one day,
you will be in someone else's arms,
and they will look at you
and wonder why you smell
like a storm is coming.

## A Day in Bed

It is the silly conversations.
It is the unspoken things,
the glance across a room,
the subtle nod of a head,
the touch of their hand
against yours.

These are the things
that I miss the most.

Nothing is silly
or small
in the end.

## A Campfire

I put up photographs
across the walls of my room
in the hope that some of that light
would shine through,
but when you capture light, it dies.

You cannot hold on to
who you want someone to be
without making them something
they're not.

It kills them because each of us
is made of a different kind of light
and we all shine in different ways.

And we all deserve our light.

IV

In which we
find each other,
again.

## A Person Who Matters

You can forget how to love.

You can be alone for so long
and be so out of practice
that your heart doesn't know
how to do what it was built for
anymore.

And it takes someone special
to teach you how to love again
and how to let the light back in.

It takes someone amazing.

## A Light in a Window

"After now,
after we've broken
everything,
what do we do?"

We turn off the light
so we can be only
what we feel.

We turn off the light
so we can be who we really are,
even if it's just until the sun comes up.

And we can be real until then.

## A Sermon

Sometimes you are ready
for each other,
sometimes not.

All you can do
is try to let each other be
who you each need to be
in the moments you have
together.

## A Hand Made of Water

We don't know
if something is meant to be.

All we can do is try
because if we do not try,
then that is not life.

And so we must try.

## A State of Being

I will become a plant that only grows in certain
parts of the world at certain times. I will become
a bird no one's ever seen before and I will be born
and die without anyone ever knowing I existed. I
will become a secret memory in someone's head, a
surprising thought that they do not understand and
they won't know where it comes from. I will become
rising strings in a song, in the background of your
favorite movie when two people kiss. I will become
the little scrunched up receipt at the bottom of
your bag and I will become the packet of sugar you
rip open when you have coffee at your favorite café.
I will become the moon and I will become the light
shining through the leaves of the tree you climbed
when you were young. I will become one beat of your
heart, and it will be the best I've ever been.

A Lion Going to Sleep

If you can,
hold my hand
and tell me
how much
this still matters.

## A Cloud of Dust

Even when I am turning away,
trust me that
I am turning toward you.

Everything is backward
because that's the way I was made.

Your sunset is my sunrise
and in a strange twilight,
we can always be together.

## An Empty Chair

They come back
and you are changed
because now you know
that you can lose them.

They come back
and everything is different now
because the world as it is
has been given a second chance.

And as much as they come back to you,
you come back to them.

## A Broken Compass

My body's facing south
so why is my heart and soul
facing north?

## A Cloud Coming Down a Mountain

I wrote this to let you know
if you ever get better,
I'll be waiting for you
on the other side.

I'll wait,
to show you
I was right
and you were strong,
in the end.

## A Quiet Night

We are chapters apart now in the book,
and the ending has always been written
the way it was written then.

But maybe in other books
that we cannot see or know,
our stories are different there.

A Tunnel of Light

Say you'll come with me.

Because I will burn this all down
for a chance to start again,
with you.

## A Face in the Crowd

I promised myself
I would never love
anyone ever again
and you have made
me break that promise.

And I have never been happier
to make a liar of myself.

A Breeze in Autumn

And God knows now
there are very few,
if any
perfect things
in this world,
but you are one of them.

## A Flower in a Book

There is a softness here
that I don't know how to climb out of,
and I am trying to tell the part of me
that wants to climb out
to stay, to calm down, that this is real now—
that two people can find each other
after they've been hurt
and heal each other
just by being with each other.

A Broken Telescope

Tell me you know me.

Tell me you understand me
in some fundamental way
that no one else ever has.

Pull my mask from my face
and name the stars you see
on the other side of me.

I have never been able
to see myself in a mirror
but maybe you can.

A Swimming Pool

The space between us is
just the surface of the water
and I can blow all the air
out of my lungs and sometimes
I pretend I live here for a while
in the loud quiet at the bottom.

Until my lungs burst
and my legs kick me back up
because my body and my mind
only ever listen to my heart
up until a point.

And then, like air, they look for you.

## A Necklace Your Mother Gave You

The only way
to truly love someone
is to love them
like you've never loved anyone else
in your life.

Or least, try.

Or just pretend.

## A Color You Cannot See

There are trees
that don't decay
in Chernobyl
because of the radiation.

We can pray
our hearts
will be the same.

## A Change

I have loved other people.

But none like you.

I have been other people.

But none like I am now.

V

In which we hope.

## A Brief Reminder

There will be a day after.

There will be a day
when you wake up and your first thought
isn't about this.

There will be a day
when you open the door, and you walk out,
without once worrying about this.

There will be a day
when the thing you think about the most
is completely and utterly unrelated to this.

There will be a day after this one
and the luckiest among us will notice it
for what it is.

A Bell at the Bottom of a Pond

Somewhere inside of you,
there's hope and a voice
waiting to say
better things.

Waiting to tell
the truth.

## A Closed Blind

People fuck us up,
and it is up to us
to find the way
back to ourselves.

And you owe it to yourself
to walk.

A Burst of Light

Here you are,
alive.

And yet there are people
who don't believe in miracles.

An Exit

Look at your worry
and say,

"Thank you for bringing this
to my attention.

You can go now."

## A Distant Grace

Even if some part of you
thinks you're not good enough,
when someone says the same,
do not mistake their cruelty
for honesty.

### A Forest

Remember all of those
who said you would never bloom
when they come to seek shade
beneath your leaves.

## A Room

We will find our way

to the other side

of the dark,

to the place

where I am not alone

in my room,

anymore

than you are

alone

in yours.

A Gentleness

Out here,
far away from everyone,
I don't feel like I know
anyone anymore,
and I feel like
I'm meeting myself
for the first time.

## An Infinite Beach

From your greatest grandfather
to a child you will never meet,
who will fly through space
and see up close
the lights you saw at night,
he or she will look back and say:

We were all here once.

# A Thing You Cannot Point At

Before your children came,
they were told that you would love them,
so whatever you do, however you treat them,
to them, it is love.

If you are cruel to them,
they will think it is love.
If you yell at them,
they will think it is love.
If you neglect them,
they will think it is love.
If you walk away from them,
they will think it is love.

And if you are kind to them,
they will think it is love.

And if you are gentle with them,
they will think it is love.

And if you listen to them,
they will think it is love.

And if you hold them tightly,
they will think it is love.

Because we cannot point
at anything that exists and say,

"This is love,"

so you will teach your children
every day they are with you what it is.

And one day, when someone else treats them
the way you treated them, they will say,

"This is love."

So teach them well.

No matter what you were taught yourself.

A Good Lie (The Only One)

Even if it's not true,
you hold their hand and
you look them in the eyes,
and you say,

"It's all going to be OK."

Because we all need that
when we're small.

# A Way to Touch the Future

Hug your children.

Because when you hug them, you are hugging everyone they will ever be. You are hugging them on their first day of school and their last. You are hugging them when they get their first promotion, when they get fired, and when they don't know how they'll pay the rent.

You are hugging them when someone says "I love you" on their wedding day and when someone breaks their heart. When you hug your children, you are hugging them when they are in the dark and when they are lost and when they are not sure how they'll get home.

When you hug your children, you are hugging them forever. You are hugging them here, and you are hugging them on the day after they cannot hug you anymore and every day after that one.

So hug them.
Hug them tightly.
And hug them a little bit longer
than you need to.

## A Chalkboard

I will not teach my children lessons.

The world will teach them all the lessons they need.

It will teach them frustration, worry, and heartache.

It will explain how hunger and anger work.

On billboards,
it will show them all the things they cannot have.

No one can live in the world and not learn these lessons.

So my job is just to be there each day
when the lesson is over.

And my job is to help them survive
the things they feel.

And I will not be cruel for the sake of a lesson.

I will be compassionate, and patient, and kind.

And that is the only lesson I will teach.

A Collection of Hope

We are different.

We are allowed.

We are loving
and we are loved.

This is what family means.

### A Voice from Your Past

You are your parents' voices,
ringing in your ears,
so be careful when you speak to a child,
your voice will echo for years
and years.

## A Rhyme and a Reason

When you look at me
and think that I'm not trying,
that is when
I'm trying my hardest.

**A Moment in Forever**

Now.

Here.

This.

## A Cloud in a Dark Sky

Be the one
who flew on.

### A Home

This is a house
of many beginnings
and second chances.

## A Bag of Stars

Maybe you are not a part of things
the way other people are a part of things,
because not everything in the universe
can be held.

## A Celestial Trade

Love is the essence

of who we are,

and so when we love,

we are both giving

a part of ourselves away

forever

and using something

that can never run out.

A Time to Decide

First,
ask yourself
if this is who
you want to be
and if the thing
you're about to do
is moving you closer
or further away
from that person.

## A Book on a Table

You have decided
that you cannot get out of bed today,
and so your outside voice says,

"Look what a terrible person I am!"

And it's loud, so you can't hear
the soft voice that says,

"This is what I need right now."

Unless you give yourself the quiet
you need, to hear.

## A Clock Striking Twelve

You are looking for the quiet,
late at night in secret small places
that only you can call your own.

You are looking for the place
that only belongs to you,
after everyone else has gone to sleep,
as you fight the nightly battle
between getting enough sleep
and getting enough time.

You are looking for yourself
and I want you to know,
it doesn't matter if you find you.

It only matters that you look.

## A Sound in the Distance

Even when you are living a life
you did not mean to live,
who you really are
is always calling.

## A Conversation with the Self

"I forgive you.
I forgive you
for needing help.
I forgive you
for not always being 100 percent.
I forgive you
for not being perfect at everything
and for not being further along
than you wanted to be.
I forgive you for feeling insecure
about whether or not you ever 'make it'
—and even if you don't,
even if your entire life
sometimes feels like
one big colossal failure,
I forgive you for that too.

I forgive you, for being human."

A Moment on the Edge

You're still obsessed
with what makes you weak,
instead of all the things
that make you strong.

You keep looking at a list going:

"Here, this happened to me,
and that makes me weak,
and this makes me weak,
and this makes me weak."

Instead of:

"These are the things
that I had to beat, and
because I had to overcome them,
I am stronger than anyone
who has not had to overcome
these same things."

## A Figure Walking Past

As long as you make
the person you are fighting against
a demon,
you will fight demons.

## A Bird Circling Up

Because the world can be terrible
and cruel, we must be kind and gentle.

Where it hurts, we must heal.

Where it takes, we must give.

Where it destroys, we must build.

Where it divides, we must join.

Not in spite of these things
but because of them.

## A Line at a Time

I was writing this poem when the teacher
told me it was the end of the test and I
was writing this poem when my mother died.

I was writing the poem when my son was
born and on the way to the hospital,
I was underlining the most important bits.

I was writing the poem when the water
dried up and when the lights went out.

And now, with the army in the streets, I
am still writing the poem.

Because the poem is my daughter, and
sunlight and my hands and the blue of the
ocean.

And when I die, when they bury me and
when my children's children's children do
not know my name,
I will still be writing this poem.

## A Way to Travel

Tell me what matters to you
so that when you are done
and dusted, dead and gone,
you are not gone.

Tell me something
that means so much to you
that if I tell it to someone else,
it is a way for you to travel
beyond the grave,
into the hearts of strangers.

## A Light

You cannot hurt me.

You cannot burn fire

or drown water.

# A Note Under a Pillow

There's a point in every movie, usually about
thirty minutes before the end, when the hero
is defeated in some truly spectacular way,
beaten into submission and presumed dead.
If not dead, then maybe they've given up and
there doesn't seem to be any way to convince
them to carry on and reach the thing they've
been reaching for.

But then, something incredible happens. They
look inside themselves and discover something
they thought was lost—the strength to carry
on. A single spark lights a fire inside them
and they return to the fight and this time
they win and the credits roll.

We tell ourselves this story again and again
because it is what we want—in our darkest
hour, we want to believe that something
inside of us, some undiscovered or forgotten
part, will help us look up from the dirt and
rise to fight again.

If you are in the dark right now, remember
that this might be the part where you have to
get up and fight.

I know it's hard to get up again and again
and again but this is what life asks of us—
to get up one more time.

I am asking you, whatever you're struggling
with right now, to get up and fight. You
might have to get up and fight again tomorrow
but that's not important now.

You'll only get there if you get up and fight,
today.

Go.

### A Bright Forest

We do not plant trees.

We plant seeds.

Give yourself
the time you need.

## A Twisting Chain

We hold on to these things so tightly that we
think that they are a part of us, and if we
do not have them in our hands constantly, we
might not be us anymore.

We hold onto grudges, past relationships,
beliefs about ourselves, and other people.
We hold onto hate and frustration and the
story we tell about ourselves.

"I am this good and no better; I am only ever
allowed to feel this specific way. I am here
in the story, and this story will repeat
itself because this is who I am."

The truth is this: The more you let go of
and give out, the more you will discover.

The person who you could be is waiting for
you to let go of the person who you are.

# A Dune in the Desert

You forget: We breathe like history breathes,
in ups and downs.

When you breathe,
which breath is the bad breath?
The inhale or the exhale?

      The tide comes in, the tide goes out;
         which waves are the bad waves?

In the light and shade of every picture,
which light is the bad light?

      When you live, which day is the bad day?

Everything
is a part of
everything else
and you
are a part of it too.

A Moth's Wing

You've spent so long
pretending you weren't hurt,
you forgot that you were,
so now you're wondering why it hurts,
and then blaming yourself
for hurting.

A Puzzle Piece Under a Couch

And just think
how miserable our lives would be
if our happiness depended entirely
on the things that happen to us.

However small,
there are parts of us
that we still get to choose.

A Ghost Rising

My life has fit me
like two left shoes.

And I am alive
with light
and defiance.

**A Small Thing That Matters**

Whatever you had to fight
to get to today,
it was worth it
to have you here.

A Crack in the Ice

Remember:

Even after all this,
you are beautiful
and your heart is pure.

A Forgotten Song

You give

and you give

and you give

not because

you have more to give,

but because

you have forgotten

how to stop giving.

## An Old Path

When you get to the top
and when you look
down,
you will not remember
a single thing that
hurt you.

## A Silver Light

Even if no one else does,
the moon sees you working.
She sees you moving in silence
to some beautiful song only you can hear.

## A Person in the Dark

At any point,

you can close your eyes

and make the only real decision that matters—

You can decide to love

and accept yourself for who you are.

You can decide to love

and accept yourself for failing.

You can love

and accept yourself for not being the person

you think you're supposed to be.

You don't have to buy anything,

go anywhere, or accomplish anything to do this.

All it requires is that you close your eyes and

decide that you are enough as you are.

So close your eyes.

A Moment in Infinity

No matter what happened today,
you grew
and you grew toward the sun.

## A Supernova

If you are standing in the dark

then stand

like you are the only light

in the

whole

fucking

universe.

## A Vector

Sometimes
you are sad and yet
here you are,
a miracle in your own skin.

A magic trick.

A purpose and direction,
made flesh.

Look at you.

## A Small Ringing Bell

When I work, I ask myself,

"If I died now,
would what I'm working on be good enough?
Would I be happy for this
to be the last thing I make?"

When I eat, I ask,

"How would this taste
if I knew I would never taste it again?"

When I spend time with my family, I ask myself,

"If something happened to me tonight,
would they know that I loved them?
Did I show them I loved them
by the way I touched them?
By the way I spoke to them?"

My goal is not to distract myself
so that I forget that I'm going to die.

My goal is to remember each day that I will.

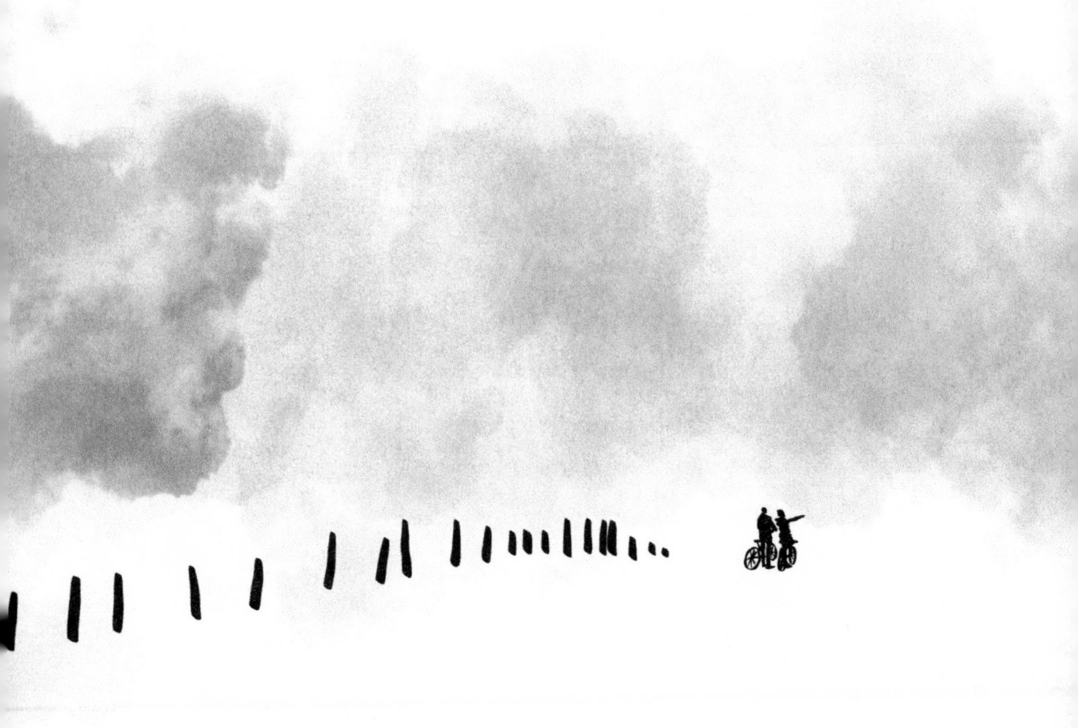

A Hospital Room in Winter

You think this is
too much to feel
but here you are—
alive and feeling this.

A Handprint on a Window

There is a kind of secret strength.

It lives in you and no one,
not even you, knows it's there.
It lives inside of you,
waiting for the day it's needed,
waiting for the darkest hour
of the darkest night.
And then, when you are defeated,
when your heart is so broken
you don't know if it can ever
be put back together again, it whispers,

"Hello. You don't know me. But I am here."

A Bandage Made of Music

We grow into our scars.

Until they disappear
into our wrinkles.

Until we only know us,
as us.

## An Island

Tell them,

I am still out here,
writing the song
I cannot sing.

A Squall

You see the storm

and think
that you are the boat

but you are the ocean

and you are the storm.

A Photograph of the Sky

You keep asking
if you're enough
even though
the well echoes back
with every coin
you throw in:

You are.

You are.

You are.

# A Footprint on a Clean Floor

Here are the rules
to the only game I play:

Every time I take care of myself,
I win a point.

Every time I stay true
to who I believe I really am,
I win a point.

Every time
I am kind.

Every time
I choose love over fear.

Every time
I am conscious of myself
in the moments that matter.

At the end of the day, I count my points,
and since I am the only one playing,
none of them matter at all
and I win.

A Noisy Neighbor

This is what I know now:

If you do not talk about your problems
in the good times,
you will yell about your problems
in the bad times.

A Rock in a Stream

You may try to move me,
but you will only move
yourself.

You will move mountains
before you move me an inch.

## A Songbird

You are angry
because your heart
isn't listening.

But your heart wasn't meant
to listen to you.

You were meant to listen to it.

And the more you listen
to your heart,
the more it will speak.

## A Red Alarm Clock

One day you will wake up

and realize

that you,

and no one else,

get to decide

what your success looks like.

## A Line in the Sand

When you have changed
the course of a river
by yelling at it,
when you have stopped the
rain from falling
with your anger,
when you have bullied a
mountain
into moving,
then you may come
and try to change me.

# A Crack in the Sidewalk

Do the difficult thing.

Not the easy thing.

The easy thing will let you live but the difficult thing will kill you, unless you kill it first.

Find where the difficult thing hides, in its difficult cave, in the difficult dark.

Then take your knife, and stab it in its stupid, difficult heart.*

Now paint your face in its difficult blood.

Walk out into the light after the long, difficult night, and show the world what horrible damage you have done.

Let them fear you.

Because you are the difficult killer.

\*Get out of bed. Take care of yourself. Write one
sentence. Write the sentence after that. Talk to
someone. Go to the thing you said you'd go to.
Avoid doing the thing you said you wouldn't.
Open the curtains. Go to bed when you planned to.
Forgive people who don't deserve to be forgiven and
then forget them. Look in between the cracks to
find the reasons why you are. Eat. Let go of what
you need to let go of. Get on the train. Answer/
avoid your emails.

Do just one thing that moves you closer to being
the person you want to be.

## A Printer's Tray

I feel the sun
on my back as I walk away
from the things
that have hurt me.

A Traffic Light in the Rain

Pain travels
until it reaches the person
who can look at it and say,

"No further. What was done to you,
you did to me. But I will not do it
to someone else."

And these people
are the reason
the world is infinitely better
than it should be.

## A Field in Winter

If you can,
think of every single thing
moving in the universe right now
and then remember
you are a part of all that.

You turn, as the universe turns.

# A Cloud in Front of the Moon

There's this idea that we are on a journey in our lives, and in that journey there is a star that we must follow.

But you will not follow one star your whole life.

There will always be a part of yourself that says,

"No, we decided on this star, we've invested so much of ourselves! We must follow it wherever it goes!" and another part of you that says,

"This just isn't working anymore. Now that I'm here, I don't know if here is right."

Changing your mind is OK. Changing who you are is OK. Changing where you want to go and who you want to be is a fundamental, important part of life.

A good life is about finding the next star and understanding that each morning, you need to wake up and ask yourself,

"Which star do I need to follow today?"

I hope you persevere when you must but also always find the courage to change course when you need to. In your life you will travel a long distance, and you will follow many stars along the way.

May they all guide you to who you were meant to be.

## A Porcelain Figure

Sometimes, being strong
just means
being stronger
than the moment you're in.

## A Passing Storm

You have a season.

You are part of a something
that moves in circles.

It comes and goes.

You are part of something,
and that is hard to remember
when where you are feels like forever.

This is not forever.

This is only now.

The seasons change.

And change again.

You get another chance.

A Toy Car

Come back
to the good in you.

It is waiting for you
to remember it.

A Star Exploding

Trust yourself.

Even when no one else does.

Even if trusting yourself
means closing your eyes
and holding your breath.

## A Gray Stone in Winter

You are not strong
until you have been given something to hold
that you do not believe you can hold,
but you hold it anyway.

A Statue Outside a Church

Even when the world
takes everything else from you,
even when you are left with nothing.

Keep yourself, for you.

## A Fish Leaping from the Water

In your mind is a river.

The river is beautiful and sunlight glints off the ripples that run across it. Perhaps it's the most beautiful river you've ever seen. As you watch the river, occasionally a fish will rise to the surface. Sometimes it is a beautiful fish, and sometimes it is an ugly fish. Sometimes the fish is large, sometimes it might seem bigger than the river itself. Sometimes there are many small fish that dart in and out of the water as it runs. Some of the fish have names like "Something I Need to Fix," "Exciting New Thing," "The One Thing I Need to Make Me Happy," "Something I Need to Do Later," "Why Doesn't This Person Love Me," or "The Thing That Is Actually Wrong with Me."

It is very easy to look at all these different fish in all their different colors and sizes and get so lost in them. You may get scared or excited by one of the fish and run along the bank of the river to try and keep up with it (or run away from it), you might wade in and try to hold it in your hand and you may even succeed in that for a while. But in no way and at no point have you ever actually been a fish and at no point will you become one.

Yet, many of us get so concerned with these fish that swim past that we think we're them, and they're us. But we're not.

We're sitting on the bank of a river in the sun.

It is hard to remember this.

Watch a child play with a toy car—what sound does the child make? It makes the sound of the engine because in the child's mind, the child IS the car. He (or she) has become the thing he is holding. This is what we do. We think we are our depression. We are our Exciting New Project. We are our If This Person Loves Me Everything Will Be OK.

But we're not.

You and I are just sitting on the edge of a river.

## A Wave

The people who need your help
are often too tired to ask for it.

Offer it anyway.

Drowning doesn't
always look
like drowning.

A Hundred Years

A true friendship transcends time.

It is one long
beautiful conversation
that stops and starts over the years
and if you are lucky
it lasts a lifetime.

## A Long Shadow

Stand up.

Not because you are called
to stand up
but because others may need
to see you stand
before they do.

## A Concentric Circle

You are not just your mind,

you are your body.

And you are not just your body,

you are the space around you.

And you are not only that space,

you are your community

and the people in it.


Cast your heart farther and farther out.


Because you will never feel safer and

more self-assured than when you fully accept

that you are not alone, that you are part of some

fundamentally magical, beautiful, living firework

that we call everything.


You belong here.


You are meant to be here.

## A Bowl of Water

We come into the world
and think
we have been taken,
and so we think,
we must take.

But this is not true.

We were given.

And so, we must give.

## A Confession

It may not seem like much,
but I promise you
in the grand scheme of your life,
every single hour
and every seemingly boring,
mundane thing in it
will be as precious as jewels one day.

## A Game

I am looking for myself
and I am trying not to yell
in case I scare myself away.

I am looking for myself
and at first I panicked
and I chased me
and I heard myself running
farther and farther away.

I am looking for myself
in the places I once knew
in the person I used to be,
but when I reach out,
I stretch like shadows stretch.

I am looking for myself
and I have to believe I will be found
when I want to be.

So I am waiting
for me
to come to me.

## A Way Through

I hope you can find some acceptance
for something
in your life today,
whatever that is,
and just allow it to be
whatever it needs to be
and let it take however long
it needs to take.

Wherever you're going,
you will get there.

## A Lullaby

Write it down
to let it leave your body
and to keep it forever
at the same time.

## A River

I write to
remind you
of the truth
because it doesn't last.

It floats away
like petals in a stream
and each day we must
find it again and say,

"This is beautiful.
This is beautiful."

We forget and,
each day,
we must remember.

A Strip of Light Under a Door

It's late at night and
you are still looking
for a reason to matter
more than you already do.

They could hold up a million signs
and write it in fireworks
they could tattoo it across
every inch of your skin
they could print it in a book
and they could yell it from tall buildings
and you still wouldn't believe them.

You need to try.

## A Galaxy

Do not ask the universe
for permission to move.

Tell it,

"I will move."

And it will carry you
to where you must go.

## A Silver Door

Sometimes,

you have to write

like you're trying

to guide someone

out of a burning building,

because sometimes,

for some people,

you are.

## A Final Glance

One must wonder at a funeral,
when someone says,
"They lived a good life."
How hard each of those letters
must have been to write.

## An Echo in the Dark

Let me die like I was born.

Memories slowly descending into the dark.

Let me forget the last few hours I won't need.
Let me wake up, surrounded by family.
Let me forget how to talk
and forget how to see;
let me forget all hurt,
and then,
let me be.

## A Bird Flying Home

A book takes a small part of me and it gives it to you and now, there is a land we share between us.

And I thank you for traveling here.

And no matter how absurd the rest of the world is right now, we must try to build a place here, in this shared land, that matters. This book can be a place we can return to when the world gets too much, a place you will always be welcome.

And one day, across a field whose length contains the universe, I will wave at you as you pass, and tell the air between us:

I see the truth of you.

And it is complicated, tragic, and always beautiful.

Always,

—Iain S. Thomas

Andrews McMeel Publishing
a division of Andrews McMeel Universal
1130 Walnut Street, Kansas City, Missouri 64106

www.andrewsmcmeel.com

21 22 23 24 25 BVG 10 9 8 7 6 5 4 3 2 1

ISBN: 978-1-5248-6044-8

Library of Congress Control Number: 2020945446

Editor: Allison Adler
Art Director: Holly Swayne
Production Editor: Amy Strassner
Production Manager: Carol Coe

ATTENTION: SCHOOLS AND BUSINESSES
Andrews McMeel books are available at quantity discounts with bulk
purchase for educational, business, or sales promotional use. For information,
please e-mail the Andrews McMeel Publishing Special Sales Department:
specialsales@amuniversal.com.

Enjoy *The Truth of You* as an audiobook, wherever audiobooks are sold.